MEL BAY'S GETTING INTO......... BLUES VIOLIN
by MARTY LASTER

CD CONTENTS

1 2 3 4 5 6 7 8 9 0

Visit us on the Web at www.melbay.com — E-mail us at email@melbay.com

Table of Contents

Introduction

Until recently, the blues was rarely taught in a formalized way, certainly not in written form. The ideas in this book (and CD) can act as a shortcut in turning you into a blues/swing violinist, but two other elements from the "old school" need to be added:

1) Listen to lots of music, played both by violinists and other instrumentalists. This can be on recordings and/or live music. Find things that you like and listen until they become a part of you.

2) Jam with others on your level and pick the brains of those more experienced than yourself. Try to form a band, while experimenting shamelessly with your own ideas. Remember that breaking the rules is often the key to great art. Otherwise, the music may sound correct but sterile. Eventually it will all make sense, but in the meantime enjoy your journey with patience and perseverance. Give it a couple of years and then reap the fruits of your labor.

In this book, there are musical ideas that are common to all instruments that fall under the category of *style*. On the other hand, there are ideas that are "violinistic"; that is, they fall naturally under the fingers and bow arm of the fiddler. I will give exercises for both. We'll also honor the great players of the past and present.

We will touch on many styles that have blues influence and in particular, how the scales and licks change depending on the expressive needs of the music.

There is lots of "stuff" in this book. Pick and choose what you need, and try not to feel overwhelmed. On this CD are tunes, breaks and the more complex exercises from the book. Lisa Gutkin is the violinist and she did a great job. The violin is favored in one channel, so you can adjust it, based on your needs.

Well, enjoy your journey and, take it S L O W....

The Violin and the Blues - an overview

To many people, the violin is not considered a blues instrument. Perhaps it is the association to classical music, strongly associated with the western European culture. Or perhaps, it is the domination of the guitar and harmonica associated with the music. The violin had its heyday as a blues/ragtime instrument in the mostly black string bands of the 1920s - 40s.

As the southern black culture moved North (specifically Chicago) and the blues became electrified and commercialized, the violin for the most part, dropped out of the picture. This is unfortunate, in my opinion. The expressive qualities of the instrument, with its ability to slide in and out of notes, makes it akin to the human voice and a potentially great blues instrument. In addition, the ability to play two notes at once is advantageous, for obvious reasons. And, regardless of one's ethnic or racial background, we all have a story to tell and emotions to express through the blues.

So, where does the violin fit in, stylistically; Delta blues, Chicago style, Piedmont, or fusion style? The answer is, all of them, but you will have to tastefully adapt your playing style to fit each one. Fusion style will allow you to be challenged technically while in Delta blues you will have to learn to say as much with fewer notes. This is sometimes frustrating for a violinist with advanced technique. You will learn to channel your technique into expressing a musical or emotional message. This may or may not be the perfect medium of expression for you.

In swing style there are role models, each of whom has (or had) virtuostic technique; Joe Venuti, Stephane Grappelli, Stuff Smith, Eddie South and Jean-Luc Ponty are among them. They all adapted their classical training to make the music swing. Swing jazz is more sophisticated as far as chordal harmonies go, but that's where I draw the line. The blues is equally challenging on a musical level and takes a subtlety and intensity of expression that is challenging in a different way. You need to find the best medium of expression for yourself, but there is so much overlapping of styles these days, try to be well versed in all of them. Enjoy the small steps in your development and you will wake up one morning and reap in the rewards of your hard work.

Minor Pentatonic Scale

For the sake of ear training we will start with the easiest scale related to the blues -- the minor pentatonic. It's a 5-note scale, without any half steps. The intervals as they relate to the 7 note minor scale are 1-3-4-5-7. In this order, I will:

1) show you the scale in several keys.
2) give you a melody that uses the scale.
3) introduce rhythmic patterns to use with the scale.
4) have you do ear training with the CD.

Practice these scales until they become second nature. Developing "finger memory" is important as you begin to rattle off the scales without thought, perhaps while watching TV.

Melodic Use of the Pentatonic Scale

These melodies use the chords on the previous page as a progression. Again, our goal is to make improvising over these scales effortless.

Now, with the same chord progression we'll add more rhythmic patterns.
Brackets show the patterns.

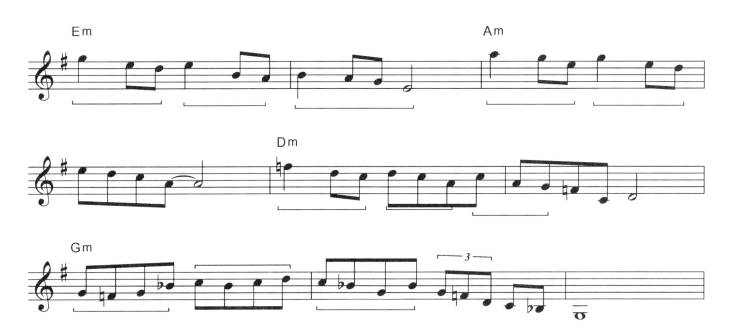

Let me introduce you to these patterns in more detail.
You should practice them with all the different blues scales in this book.
The notes will change but the formula for each pattern stays the same.
I will stay on the Em pentatonic. It's up to you to transpose to the other keys.

4-note patterns

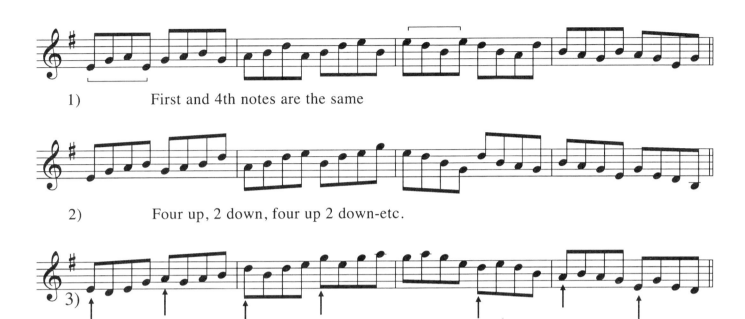

1)   First and 4th notes are the same

2)   Four up, 2 down, four up 2 down-etc.

3)

First note in each group of four is a 4th higher than the previous one. This one works best with this minor pentatonic scale.

Three-Note Pattern - This is just one example for now so you can get your feet wet.

Three up - One down

Ear Training

Ear training is an essential part in your development as an improviser. Some of us need it more than others and you'll know where you stand fairly quickly. Study the intervals below. We are dependent on our ability to recognize them in order to play back or write (transcribe) what we hear. These are the easiest but are the building blocks for the more complex intervals. Learning to hear these will make "picking up" licks much easier. We'll begin with an A for tuning (on CD - track 1). This next excercise is on track 2.

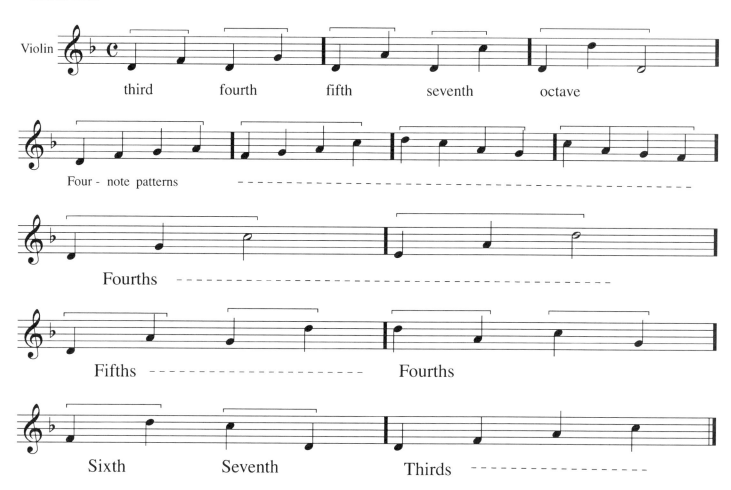

Mimic what you hear on the CD, taken from the above examples and not necessarily in order. I used the piano so you can get used to picking things up from instruments other than the violin. You have two chances for each. Don't look at the music. This is not a test but, --- I'LL BE WATCHING YOU!

Slidin' Around

Getting the true sound of the blues on the violin depends in part on your ability to slide your fingers in a certain way. In the classical domain, the slide (or glissando) is, for the most part, an ornament used to highlight the note being slid into. In the blues, the slide is just as important as the note you are sliding to and, at the risk of sounding like a teacher of Zen, the *journey* of the slide is what's important and gives the music it's expressive power. Have the feeling that the tips of your fingers have been dipped in butter or vaseline and they can potentially slide at any moment. Probably better advice than smearing lubricants on your fingers is to listen to great blues vocalists or guitarists. They seem to rarely land on a note and stay there for long. Try these sliding licks in different keys. For practice, don't stop the slide on one finger before going to the next. It will sound a bit like an ambulance siren if you do it correctly. Maybe you should alert your neighbors before trying this.

Quick Slides
Slower slides

This is an excercise in slower, lazy slides.

These use the quick slides.

These two-measure phrases use a combination of slow and fast slides.

9

This is a good blues tune for practicing your slides. It also introduces most of the notes you will find in the blues. We'll get more into that later. Now, just enjoy sliding and listening to these licks.

Greasy Finger Blues

Marty Laster

The **Blues Scale** differs from the minor pentatonic with the
addition of one note, the flat (♭) 5. That interval is shown with a bracket.
These are identical in major and minor keys and work great in both.

This scale is a great starting point for playing the blues. However, the scale is a
chameleon and changes its musical color depending on the "feel" and style of the particular blues tune. We will explore that later, but for now, here's the basic Blues Scale in several keys.

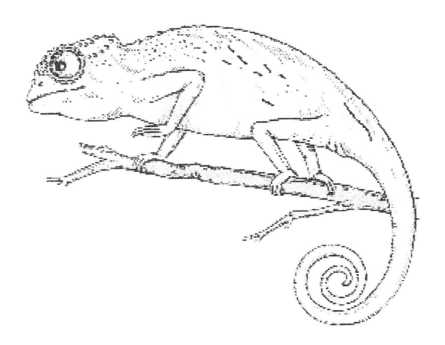

The Blues Scale

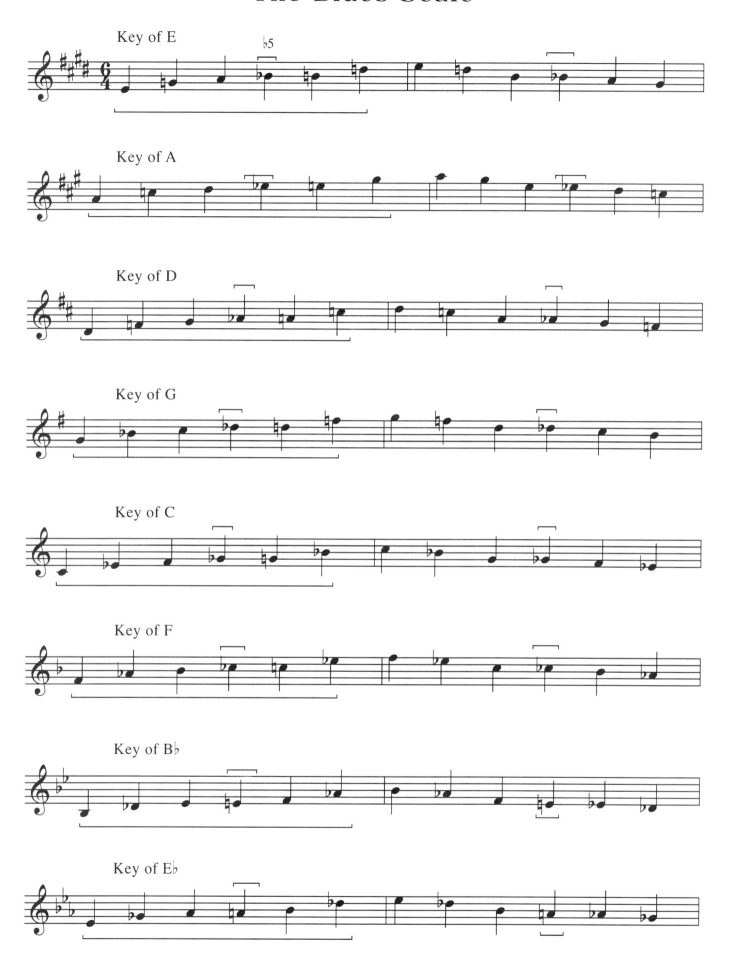

This tune begins our real study of the blues style.

The blues scale works nicely in minor keys. On this CD this tune is preceded by the blues scale in E.

Lazy Bones

Marty Laster

On the following page is a blues that uses the ♭5 interval and gives you a chance to further develop your "sliding chops."

A great example of this interval are the first three notes of "Maria" from *West Side Story*. (Dim. 5th in bracket.)

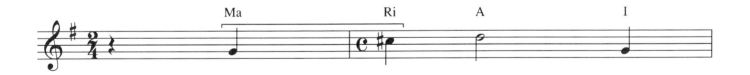

Notice that the dim. 5th in "Maria" was a G to C♯. That technically makes it a sharp 4. The sound is identical to the D-A♭ below. That's what's important to us right now.

The Roller Coaster

Marty Laster

14

Practice with Rhythm

Once I had the privilage of playing in a string workshop of African-style music. The instructor, Ken Mackintyre would often "drum" in the idea that we should approach the violin as if it were a percussion instrument with the bow being a mallet or drumstick.

This concept, that rhythm can come first and melody is secondary can have a profound influence on a classical string player trained to focus on playing with a beautiful tone, and where rhythm takes a back seat. This concept that, when improvising, you would come up with a "rhythmic lick" and add the notes almost as an afterthought was an exciting idea to me. Of course, ideally, melody and rhythm should go together but this concept may help to jump-start those who need extra work with rhythm.

Okay! Before we start improvising, let's loosen up with some rhythms. You can tap them out or play with the bow on open strings. Pay special attention to the syncopated rhythms (notes in between the beats). Fool around with your own rhythms as well. Note the quarter-note triplets in the next to last measure. Fitting three notes evenly into two beats takes some practice.

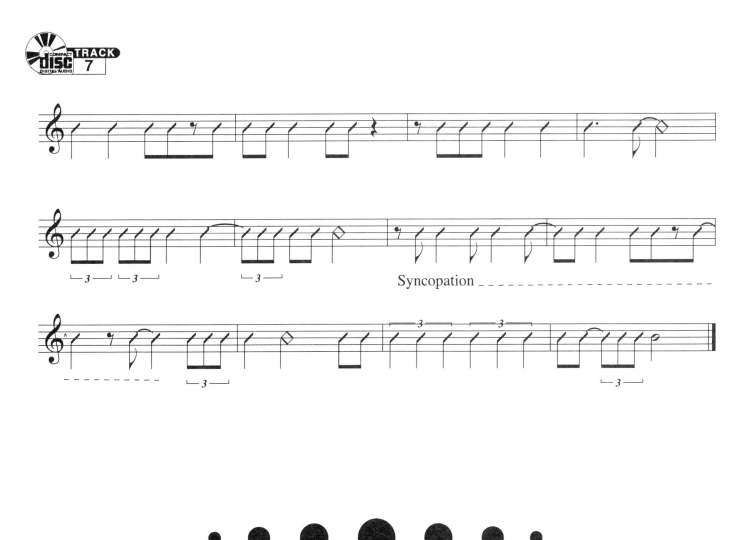

15

Now I'd like to demonstrate a few blues "licks", taken from the scale. Try to memorize and transpose them into all of the keys on the blues scale page. On the CD you will have one chance to copy each lick. Try not to look at music. This is in the key of E, one of the more popular blues keys, used quite a bit in "Chicago Blues". See if you could transcribe into G and C for starters.

(Look at bottom of page for transposing tips)

Transposing tips - Let's take lick #3 and transpose into the key of A.
Here are two ways to go about it
1) the key of A is a 5th lower (or a 4th higher) from E Simply lower or raise each note
2) Find the first note by going down a 5th (in this case, up a 4th)
Next, analyze the intervals in the lick. (This way is better for developing your ears.)

16

Now you are ready to start creating your own licks. Let begin by altering or "decomposing" lick #3.

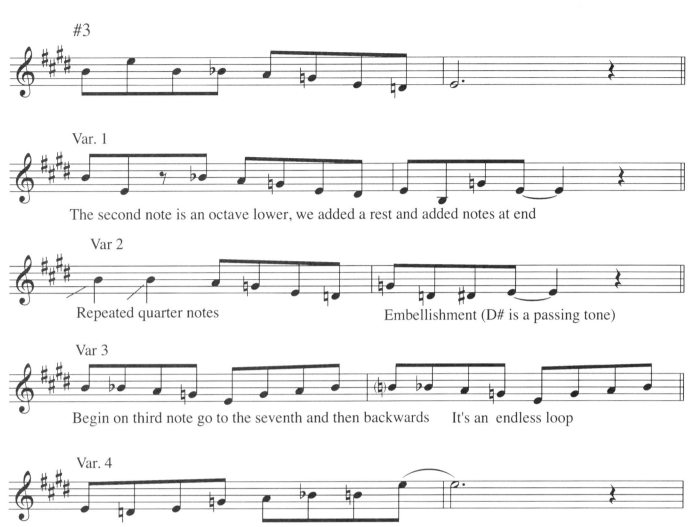

#3

Var. 1

The second note is an octave lower, we added a rest and added notes at end

Var 2

Repeated quarter notes   Embellishment (D# is a passing tone)

Var 3

Begin on third note go to the seventh and then backwards   It's an endless loop

Var. 4

This is the lick lick backwards, starting with an eighth note.

This is an old blues tune, dated before 1930. It's a great tune and an introduction to syncopation (which we'll get into a bit later.) Also, I want to show a blues in which the minor 3rd is not used at all in the melody. It is interesting that the fiddler, Howard Armstrong, played the major 7th in the first measure, even though the vocalist did not. This gives the temporary impression that this is in the key of D, instead of G. My transcription conforms to the vocal melody, however. By the way, the key of G was popular among the string bands of the '30s and '40s. This can be heard on the CD, *Violin, Sing the Blues for Me* (Old Hat Records.)

it's called ... **Travelin' Railroad Man**

18

To Change Scales or Not?

When playing the blues, we have choices, as far as the scales to use. For example, in the key of G, when moving from the G (1) to the C (IV) chord, you can continue to play the notes of the G blues scale or you can move to the C blues scale over the C chord. It is interesting how the notes of the G blues scale can work with both chords.

The ♭II and II work in the C chord as chromatic or passing tones. When moving to the D (V) chord, we must withdraw from the G blues scale into the key of D. Here are two sample improvs on "Railroad Travelin' Man". The first stays on the G blues scale until the D chord. The second changes to the C blues scale over the C chord. To keep it simple there will be a lot of repetition.

Let me point out that playing the same blues scale over two chords can work in the traditional blues or rock styles, but doesn't work as well as we enter into swing jazz and other more complex styles. Practice both styles of improvising.

Harmonica Licks

These speak for themselves. The speed and length of the trill is up to you and the ones using the 5th and 7th on top are highlighted with a solid line and those using the 7th and 9th, a dotted one.
--- Try lick at end (in E) for bending trill - It's not easy, but very cool. ---

12-Bar Blues

This is the standard progression used in the blues. There are variations to this, as we will see, but this is the simplest and the most used. Keep in mind that many blues tunes don't use this exact progression.

Trading fours - This relates to alternating your solo with other musicians, 4 measures at a time. You would play until the A chord and someone else would take over up to the B7, etc. This would usually last two times around.

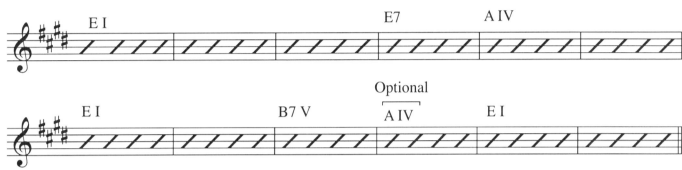

This is a chance for you to jam. Try to apply the licks from the previous page to the next CD example. Of course you will have to learn the licks in the keys of A and B, in addition to E. Experiment with your own ideas. It's time to let loose and let your imagination soar. Don't worry about taste just yet. Exploration is our goal now. In the last chapter of the book, we'll get into refining your ideas. On the CD, there is a Chicago style blues for you to jam to. The only melody is a familar repeated "vamp", and you are in the hot seat to "wail" over the chord progression. Time to get down with your bad selves.

Here's a scale I call the blues pentatonic. The traditional Major-pentatonic scale uses these intervals of the major scale - 1, 2, 3, 5, 6. As is, the scale is rarely used in blues playing so we will quickly move on to the altered versions. Notice there is no flatted 5th so it has a more country-ish, less funky feeling than our standard blues scale. Well, just when we were getting used to things, there's that chameleon to change colors on us.

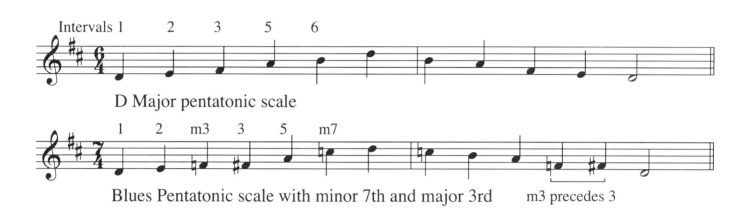

On the next page is part of a tune played by the string bands of the 40's into the present. It's called the "Dickson County Blues." The melody is in a swingy, syncopated style but the blues is definately present. After stating the melody (first half of tune), I'll add a simple improvisation using the above scales. This is an example of an 8-bar blues.

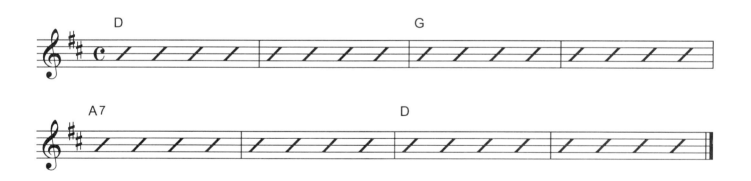

Dickson County Blues

Arthur Smith

Here are some licks in D using the blues pentatonic scale. This is beginning to touch on swing style. (We'll get into that a bit later.) On the CD you will have time to imitate each lick. Try not to look at the music.

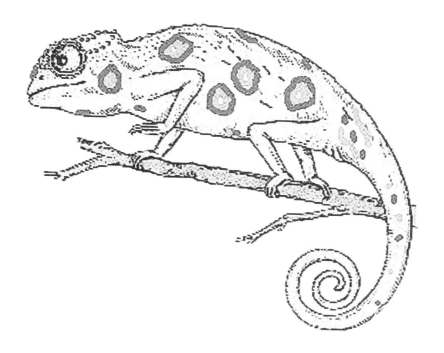

We're going to leave the string band genre and touch on the blues in the context of Western Swing style. This is an upbeat song that I believe is from the 1940s and has been recorded by countless artists. In this style you can use the blues pentatonic scale for improvisation and lean on the minor 7th of each chord with lots of sliding to bring out the blues. I included two excerpts on CD of very contrasting natures. One is from the great bluegrass fiddler, Chubby Wise, who didn't stray far from the melody but used very expressive slides. The other is Vassar Clements (*Crossing the Catskills* LP), who touches on the melody briefly and then does his thing. Here's the Chubby Wise rendition of...

Corina, Corina

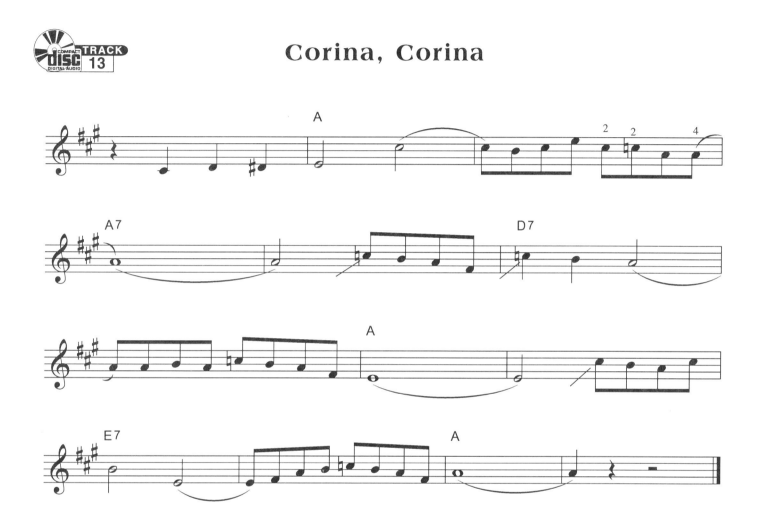

CD Track 13
"Corina Corina"
Performed by Vassar Clements from the release *Crossing the Catskills* (ROUN 0016)
Courtesy of Rounder Records
www.rounder.com

Now here's a bit of a novelty tune that was also popular in the '30s and '40s. It has a swingy ragtime progression. Because the chords change so quickly, improvising is tricky. I transcibed the basic melody without all the frills. The chord in measure 12 was a G minor on the 1930s recording, but today the B diminished is preferred. This is also on *Violin, Sing the Blues for Me*. Okay, here's...

Adam and Eve

With a tune like "Adam and Eve", where the chord changes are fast and furious, it's difficult to improvise using licks. Try using chordal tones (arpeggios) instead. Practice them in the various keys until they're second nature. These include the minor 7th and move in the circle of 5ths. (More about that later)

Here's a sample improvisation on "Adam and Eve" using arpeggios only. We'll do it in the key of B♭ as well. I put the B7 chord at beginning of the measure to give you more time.

This familiar lick (in bracket) is useful on this quick II (major) VI progression. The E7 chord uses the 9th of the scale, the F♯.

Here's the same break in B♭. Begin to come up with your own lines using the CD, using arpeggios only.

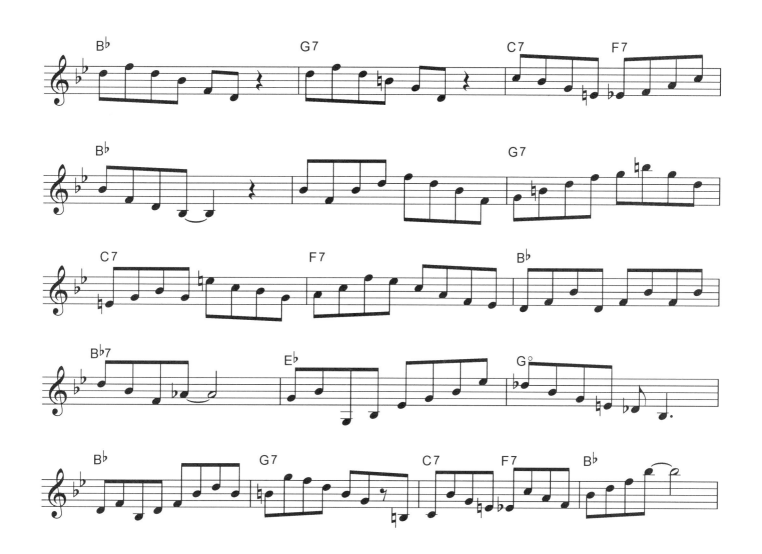

That was good practice but not very interesting, musically. This is still "Adam and Eve," but with some spicy blues intervals and passing tones added to the arpeggios (look for the S). I used the first half of the tune in both keys.

in B♭

The Mixolydian Mode

This is simply the major scale using the ♭7th. It is a cousin of the major arpeggio with the ♭7th added, as we will see later.

Try this - Go up with arpeggio and down with Mixolydian mode

Now reverse the order

Here is a transcription of an old timey tune that uses the mixolydian mode with some bluesy slides. The danger of transcribing a tune like this is that you miss the subtle variations that come with each repetition. You can hear a short sample of the tune on the companion CD, but I recommend that you get the CD, *Ways of the World* (Ruthie Dornfeld, fiddle -- Foxglove Records) to get the feel of this style. Both parts of the tune are repeated, though I faded the snippet before both repetitions. It is typical in old timey style to have measures with extra beats. Hence, the 6/4 measures.

Polly Put the Kettle On

Ruthie Dornfeld

From the CD *Ways of the World* (Foxglove Records)
Courtesy of Ruthie Dornfeld - www.ruthiedornfeld.com

Here's an example of a blues break using a mixture of arpeggios (Arp. - with solid line underneath) and mixolydian mode. (Mix. - dotted line).

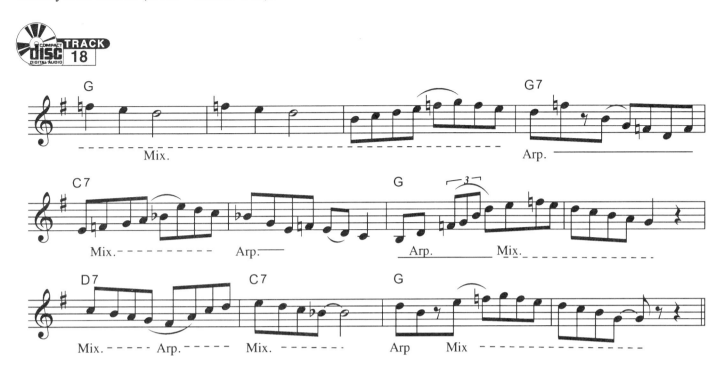

Using the same mixolydian mode, try raising the 4th to a ♯4. This exotic effect is often used in blue-grass music. Try the above blues using this change. There's that chameleon again to remind us that there are many dialects in this blues language.

Now here's the same thing using the minor third. This uses the dorian mode (raised 6th) and is used in Klezmer music.

OK! We've covered a lot of ground. Try this blues break that contains many of the ideas and techniques worked on so far. We'll call it the...

Kitchen Sink Blues

In the act of cramming so many ideas in one solo, I didn't let the music breathe. When playing an actual break, it's better to replace some ideas with rests and slides.

Here's a blues of mine that uses the minor pentatonic scale in the melody. The Dorian mode is used briefly as well. Instead of the B7 chord, try the B minor. It works just as well. This offers a form of syncopation in which notes are anticipated one eighth note early. For example,

On the beat   Anticipated

Anticipation Blues

Marty Laster

35

Rhythm - Part 2

Our tendency as a newbie improviser is to place a lick in the beginning of the measure on the downbeat. That is fine, but experiment putting the lick on different beats in the measure and it can change it's feeling and function radically. Look at the following lick. In Example #1, the lick begins on beat 1, the strongest beat and the lick acts as a unified whole. In examples 2, 3 and 4, the lick is placed in different places in the measure which creates the feeling that various notes act as a pickup into the downbeat (beat one). #5 is particularly tricky because it's all syncopated (off the beat.)

In Cajun music, you can find many tunes influenced by the blues. The improvisation is subtle and there is much use of slides and the minor 7th. Michael Doucet is probably the most influential fiddler in this style today. His band Beausoleil has recorded countless CD's and has toured the world.

This is an old standard with obvious Blues/Mixolydian roots.

Parlez Nous a Boire

On the next page, I'd like to include the first half of another popular Cajun tune. The use of the minor 7th (G natural) without other blue notes points to the Mixolydian mode as its basic structure. This is not on the companion CD.

Angelo DeCesare

Bosco Stomp

The more contemporary cousin of Cajun music is the Zydeco style. It evolved in the melting pot of the South, New Orleans, and the music reflects that, having roots in Cajun, African, Latin and mixed with the electronics of rock. The accordian dominates the average Zydeco ensemble and the music is highly improvisational. When there is a fiddle present, the style of fiddling is closer to rock/fusion than Cajun with the addition of drones. The music is very bluesy and usually uses simple chord progressions

Swing Style

The relationship between swing and blues styles vary. There is a hint of blues in most swing because of the use of the slide into the major 3rd in addition to the presence of the minor 7th. The amount of blues influence depends of course on who's playing and the period of time in history. During the big band era (1940s), the music functioned as a vehicle for dancing and was generally on the happy side. There was rarely the use of the diminished fifth and the emphasis was clearly on the swing rhythm. Moving into post big band era and into bebop style, there was a major change. The change from the tight, disciplined ensembles of the big band to a more individual approach to jazz paved the way for major changes in the music. An increase in chromaticism (non chordal notes) encouraged more bluesy ideas and the fact that artists were beginning to perform in more intimate club and bar settings set the tone for more personal expression. This proved to be fertile ground for blues and jazz musicians who were drawn to the blues.

For the purpose of our book, we will deal mainly with the simpler, older forms of swing and in the last chapter I will discuss some more advanced techniques. For our purposes, our discussion of swing improvisation will involve three general ideas:

1) Licks
2) Arpeggios using patterns
3) Scales using patterns

Swing time is rarely written out.   This is the way it's played.

Swing Licks can be created by sliding into the 3rd degree of the scale. In the key of G, it would be a B note. All the following licks are in G. On the CD you will imitate each lick. (There will be strict penalties for looking at music.)

TRACK 23

Try these chromatic licks

This is a classic lick.

Using Arpeggios

Benny Goodman was a master at making the music swing using arpeggios. Of course, he did much more than that, but I want to show how you can use this technique without it sounding like a "Kreutzer Etude." We will use patterns (shown with bracket) and then add rests and syncopation to help swing it.

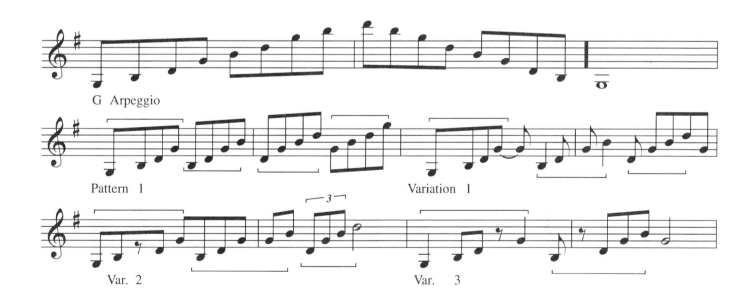

G Arpeggio

Pattern 1   Variation 1

Var. 2   Var. 3

See if you can come up with your own variations based on the following pattern:

Scales and Patterns -- Try in all keys

Major Scale   Mixolydian going down

Pattern 1   Mix. going down

Pattern 2   Mix. going down

Pattern 3   Mix. going down

Simply by changing the rhythms and adding a rest, look at how we can make pattern 3 swing.

Swing   variation on Pattern 3

Blues Chord Chart in Swing Style

The additions to the standard progresssion are bracketed

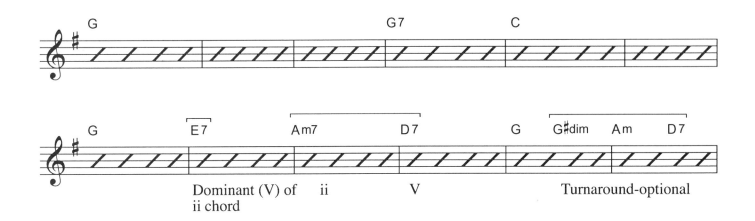

The ii - V progression has special significance in the late Swing period and especially in the bebop era. A classic use of this is the beginning of the Duke Ellington standard, "Satin Doll." The turnaround is used to move you back to the top of the progression and is not used at the end of the tune. The easiest way to improvise over a turnaround is with the use of arpeggios 1) or you could hold notes and move chromatically 2).

Here are two examples. This includes the ii - V progression:

Syncopation is a basic component of swing. The basic idea is that accented notes will fall on the offbeats or in between the beats. You can say that the notes fall in the cracks. In 4/4 time the off-beats are 2 and 4. Words can cause confusion so let's get right on to the musical examples. I used one lick and then syncopated it. Try to play the whole sequence non stop. These techniques are great for Blues as well.

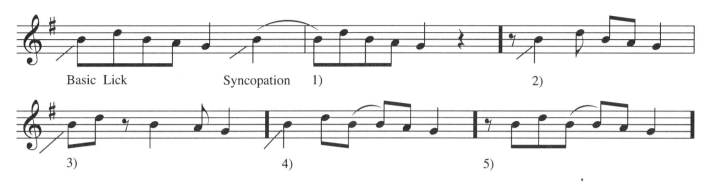

The circle of fifths is a common progression in swing. You would go a 5th down (or a 4th up) after each chord and add the minor 7th (except for the 1 chord of the key.) We will do a 4 chord circle starting on D7 and ending on F (plus a one-chord turnaround). This is a typical example of a swing improv. using all the techniques in our ever-growing arsenal of ideas. On the CD, after the following break you have an opportunity to solo in F (as written) and A♭.

The chords will be F7, B♭7, E♭7 and A♭.

Playing this with a metronome may be a good idea.

43

Bowing in Swing Style

When asked how he approaches bowing, jazz violin giant Stephane Grappelli replied in his rich Gallic tones, "well, zee bow-eet goes up - then goes down." To a natural musician like Stephane, this seems logical but to most of us mortals, it's not very helpful. I'd like to offer a couple of ideas and bowing patterns that will hopefully shed some light.

Try these patterns with scales, including the pentatonic (1, 2, 3, 5 and 6 degrees of the major scale). Make sure to practice in the flat keys (F, B♭, E♭, etc). Remember, the patterns are written as eighth notes but are played in swing time.

Bowing #1 is great for playing swing, You can use very little bow and play very smoothly and Grappelli-like. It's also a great way of keeping the bow in one spot (i.e - the middle to tip.)
IN GENERAL, the use of threes with bowing, whether with separate eighth notes or slurs, helps the music to swing, especially if you accent the beginning of each group.

There are countless ways in which the following break can be bowed. It is a personal choice and may change each time you play it. This is just to demonstrate how these three specific patterns can be used.

Using Bow Patterns in a Swing Improvisation

This is based on the opening chords of "Lady Be Good," using bowings from the previous page.
Numbers of the bowings are beneath each one used.

On the third line I implied a turnaround of substitution chords (in bracket). If the accompanist just holds a G chord, the line will sound more dissonant.

The use of bowing #2 in measure 8 is a good example of choosing a bowing to avoid slurring notes and crossing strings at the same time.

Here's an old swing tune that uses the circle of 5ths (D-G-C) and also has the I-dim ii-V turnaround and at the end, ii-V-I. Try an improvisation of your own on the

Darktown Strutters Ball

Did you notice the ii-V-I progression at the beginning of line 3? We are now leaving our chapter on swing style and it's relationship to the blues. You can see that they are not so distant cousins and at times there is a fine line that distinguishes them.

Vibrato or not? --- That is the question.

In Blues and Swing, vibrato should be used sparingly. That fast and constant throbbing classical vibrato needs to be replaced by one that ornaments the notes more on an individual basis. A nice tone is still to be aspired, but takes a back seat to rhythmic attack and creative ideas. The vibrato can now be more laid back (slower). The faster one should be reserved for the wild, untamed vibrato - forbidden in classical circles. Many players, including Stuff Smith and Papa John Creach, used this. The technique helps the music to swing and adds life to individual notes and at times, a humorous touch.

How to execute this vibrato ~
* Start the note.
* Then begin to vibrate normally.
* Almost immediately, consciously intensify the vibrato while easing off of the downward pressure of
  the finger. This will make the finger slide along the string slightly, changing the pitch a bit.
* Sustain this until the end of the note.

Warning: This wild vibrato occasionally causes the hand to actually leave the body. Watch out for these dangerous projectiles. A helmet is recommended for your protection.

Angelo DeCesare

Less is More

About playing fast:

In general, newby improvisers often play too gosh-darn quick (excuse the foul language.) Unless you are being paid by the note, take your time and be more reflective, especially in playing the blues. An important concept is to treat rests as an important part of the music. I like the description of music as being a "sound-sculpture" with the rests helping to define the notes being played. Not playing at the beginning of a measure creates tension that's released when you enter and not playing at all for a measure gives the listener a break while he/she is wondering what's coming next. Using a non-fiddler as an example, Miles Davis was a master of the less is more concept. Just listen to the recording of *Kind of Blue*.

There is definitely a place for playing fast, but it's in the context of tension and release. If you play a fast flurry of notes following a sustained slow slide, it's extremely effective. Holding back is not the same as playing without energy. Some of the most effective breaks can be when the energy is building up and ready to explode, but never does. Experiment with your arsenal of slides, trills, ways of vibrating and attacking with the bow. If you don't own those skills, than you are forced to compensate with lots of notes in order to express yourself.

Listening and creating

Listening to lots of music is a key to success as an improvising musician. Take a recorded break that you like and transcribe it (write it down.) Next memorize it. If you can do this without transcribing, all the more power to you. The key is to make the break a part of you. It should eventually feel like you created it yourself. When the ideas from the break come out in your own playing and sound simpler, don't judge it. Simpler does not mean worse. The key is to make it your own and how you next interpret your own version is the key.

Take your ideas and twist them around, turn them upside down and inside out. Make a mental note of what you like in this exploration process. Only then you begin to get in touch with your voice. The next step is choosing where to place these ideas in addition to how to build a convincing break. (To be discussed later.)

Play with people - A lot!

Practicing the scales and ideas in this book is a beginning, but falls short of really making music if done in a vacuum. Jamming and/or playing in a band that rehearses can teach us the art of laying back, taking turns with soloing, and most of all, listening. You will get to bounce your ideas off of others and hear what they have to say. Taping these sessions can be useful. It's also good to copy the sounds of unlike instruments such as electric guitar, harmonica and horns. They have a natural attack that doesn't come easy on the violin and goes against our training in producing a beautiful tone. I've yet to hear a classical teacher say; "Hey! Is that the raunchiest sound you can get"?

About that attack, place the bow on the string and without playing, assert pressure on the bow by bearing down with your forefinger. See if you can move the string without actually playing (make sure bow is rosined). Now, keeping that pressure on the string, think of a word that begins with a P. Finally, pull the bow suddenly (you're playing now). That should create the explosive attack we are looking for. This will help your classical playing as well.

For you Classical Converts (and you know who you are)

I was one myself and understand the difficult transition of morphing into an improvising violinist. After helping many violinists to convert, certain patterns have emerged.

We are trained to connect notes in a seamless way. The concept of speaking through the violin with spaces of unpredictable lengths between the notes, in addition to the attack (page 48), is new. Also discussed earlier in the book was the use of less vibrato (Page 47), to be used now as an ornament. Your refined technique is a potential asset as you crawl into your cocoon to be reborn as an improviser.

With the blues, rhythmic intensity and flexibility are now the norm. Eighth notes need not be exact metronomically, and some notes may be in the cracks, pitch wise and may no longer conform to the traditional European model. I am not endorsing sloppiness, but adapting our technique to a new musical world. What used to be an out-of-tune note is now one that screams out with emotion and a phrase that was rushing rhythmically now has an urgency to express itself. There is still discipline, but in the new context of immediacy and spontaneity of emotion. Like all music, when played well, this disciplined raw emotion seems effortless and deceptively simple. Some blues artists show their artistry with fast flurries of notes and others (BB King comes to mind), with the subtlety of the treatment of one note. The bottom line is; the blues sets off deep feelings within us, and that experience speaks for itself.

The adult fear of letting go happens when we can't accept being a beginner all over again. It is humbling that with all our technique, we cannot accomplish in a month or year what a great blues artist with no training has done in their lifetime. Practice the material in this and other books and transcribe and memorize solos that you like or are challenged by. Finally, allow a certain portion of your practice time for childlike exploration and jamming. This should be relatively free of thought and judgment, as you are internalizing all that you have learned thus far. Taping these sessions may be a good idea as you evaluate your progress at a later time.

Your classical chops will not suffer, and may in fact improve as you begin to interpret a written phrase with more rhythmic flexibility and glissandos now have a more soulful quality. Switching styles may be a temporary struggle but with practice and time, moving from Romantic to blues and back to Baroque should be effortless.

The shortcut to playing the blues (or any style) is of course, immersing oneself in the music. I have played with bluegrass, swing and blues players with limited ability who played convincingly, simply because they lived and breathed a style their entire lives. Musical language is mastered with commitment plus lots of time. And remember, practicing is important but listening and jamming is paramount.

Good luck!

Bluegrass Style

is a virtuostic blend of the Blues, old-timey fiddling styles and Irish music. It stands as an independent entity. In the traditional style, improvisation is fairly structured and doesn't stray too far from the melody, especially on vocal tunes. In the more current Bluegrass, there is more spontaneity but the language is still limited, compared to Jazz. There are bluesy licks that are quirky, the mixolydian scale is used and the interval of the 4th is utilized quite a bit, notably with the use of double stops. Also there is the use of drones -- two strings at once with the melody on one string and with the other string open. Below is a typical traditional Bluegrass improvisation over the chords of "Blue Moon of Kentucky," by Bill Monroe.

Look at that last D7 lick. It is interesting how the last 4 notes anticipate the next G chord. (Look below) This is particular to Bluegrass, but interestingly, it happens in Bebop jazz as well. Of coure, there are many more Bluegrass fiddle licks and ideas as they relate to bluegrass.

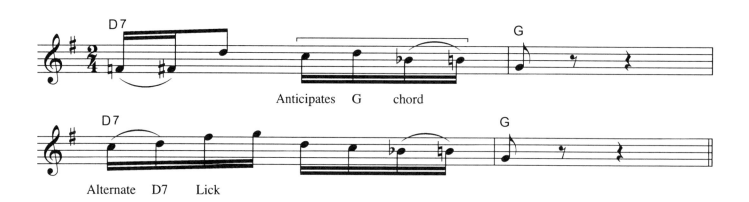

50

When accompanying in a bluegrass band, you would "chunk" or play double stops at the frog on the off beats (2 and 4). It should sound percussive.

Here's a short example, inspired by Bill Monroe's instrumental style. This should give you a feeling for the use of drones in bluegrass fiddling. In addition to, once again, the mixolydian mode.

We will end our short visit with Bluegrass style with a break to "Salty Dog Rag:"

Mixing Minor and Major chords takes some getting used to. Watch the tendency to play the Blues or other scales through all the chord changes. We will begin with the simple two chord tune:

Drunken Sailor

The simplest way to approach an improv is the Blues scale for minor and the Pentatonic for major. Notice that the chord changes are quicker at the end of the tune.

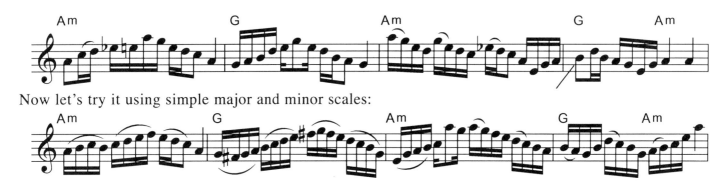

Now let's try it using simple major and minor scales:

Notice that the melody has a raised 6th, the F♯. This transforms it to the Dorian mode. This sample improv uses the Am chord in Dorian and the G chord using a variation of the Mixolydian mode. We will do two breaks on this one.

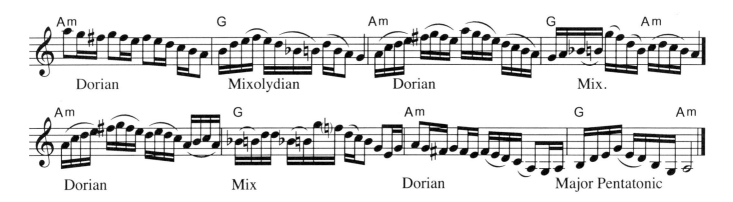

Here's a tune inspired by the great Gypsy guitarist, Django Reinhardt. The V chord (A7) in this style presents some interesting new possibilities for improvisation. Here is...

A Gypsy Dream

Now some sample improvisations. Notice the use of the ♭9th (B♭) on the dominant A7 chord. It works well in the Gypsy style but not in "Drunken Sailor." I will begin by using minor pentatonic patterns with two chords. Notice the augmented second interval in the sixth measure. This is also common in Klezmer music.

Well, just when you thought the Blues is only played with the minor 7th here comes that chameleon to change all that. This is a blues I wrote in a Gypsy style that uses the Major 7th. In the key of G minor that would be an F♯. Blasphemy, you may say, but it works.

Gypsy Blues

Marty Laster

Second Position

The use of the second position can be useful when playing the Blues, especially over the C and F chords. Here are fingerings for the various scales and licks.

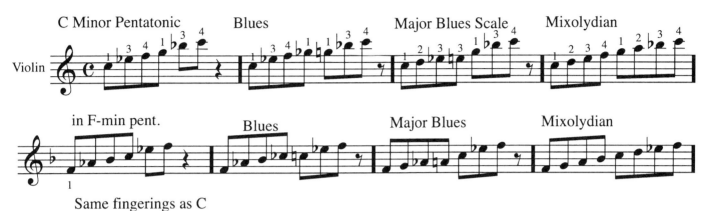

C Minor Pentatonic   Blues   Major Blues Scale   Mixolydian

Violin

in F-min pent.   Blues   Major Blues   Mixolydian

Same fingerings as C

Licks -- For the key of F, simply play the lick one string lower.
On CD, there's a rest after each measure

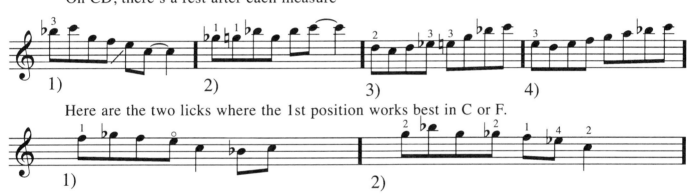

1)   2)   3)   4)

Here are the two licks where the 1st position works best in C or F.

1)   2)

Here's a part of a tune that mixes the 2nd and 1st position.

C   F

2nd Pos

C   G7

1st Pos.

55

Three Note Patterns

- These are really popular in all improvised music but playing groups of threes in 4/4 time is tricky as far as anticipating where the chord changes are. I will give you a Dm, followed by an E♭ minor chord for each example to maximize the feeling of the chord change. On CD, there's a rest at the end of each line.

1)   Three-Note Patterns

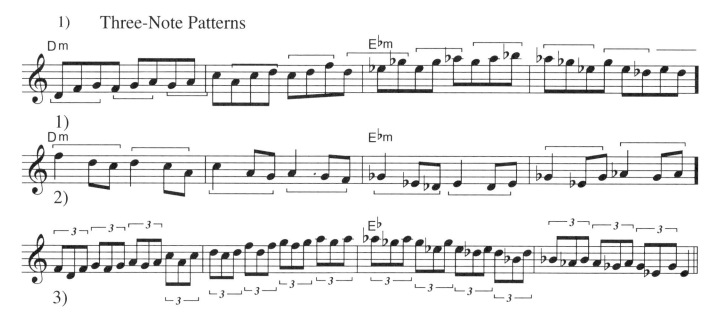

1)

2)

3)

Repeated 3-Note/Beat Patterns.

This is one of my favorite techniques; these licks act as an endless loop. Depending on the context, patterns may be played over different chord changes without changing any notes and some licks need a note altered with the chord changes. These will move from an E to an A chord.

The Next 4 measures will act as a sneak preview to the following page. The Bracket shows the three-note pattern.

Here the B(5th) becomes a 9th of the A Chord

Repeated licks continued--Brackets show the repetitions

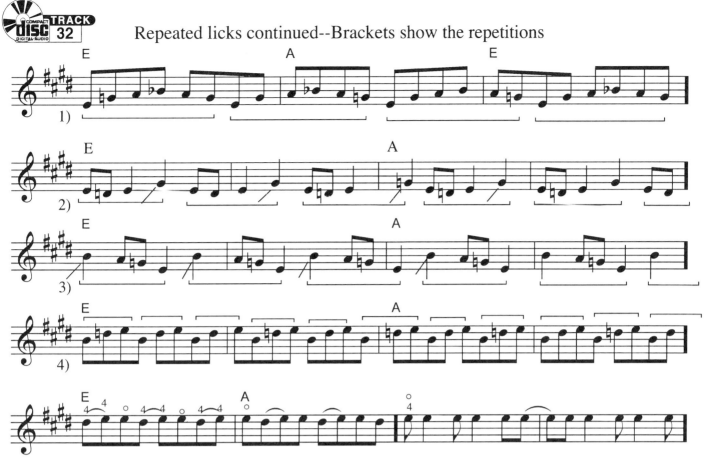

5) Try this ever popular pinky slide lick . 6) Rhythmic variation of same lick.
Play first two notes with open E string for tension.

Notice how these patterns work against all the chord changes in "Adam and Eve."

2)   3) Harmonica Lick

Warning: These patterns are to be played at your own risk. They are known to induce a dreamlike trance. I knew a fiddler once who played one of these licks non-stop for 3 days before his wife had him carted away. He continued playing it until his death two years later. Sad, but true.

Using Common Tones

It is really effective to repeat a note, going from one chord to another when it is a common tone to both chords. This relates to the repeated patterns we just did. Below is an example using "A Gypsy's Dream."

Adding more notes camouflages the idea, but we are still circling the Ds.

"Adam and Eve" is a good tune to do with this.
Sometimes when the chord changes you have to move half a step.

If you simplified the whole thing, you'd come up with the following melody.

"Dickson County Blues" is an interesting example of this. There are two things happening:
1) The D stays the same with the chord change and 2) the F♯ changes to F natural.

58

Double Stops

Sure, those sax players look pretty cool and can play quicker than we can, but we got something up our sleeves that they don't have-Double Stops (unless, of course, you're a disciple of Roland Kirk, who had the ability to play two notes at once on the sax.)

These can be difficult to master but are really effective in the Blues. I divide double stops into four categories:

--- Those that use the interval of the 3rd, 6th and 9th -- this comes close at times to classical playing in sound aside from the use of slides.

--- The use of the diminished 5th (the devil's interval.) This finger twister brings out the tension and angst of the blues

--- The unison with the 4th finger and open string -- this creates tension by beginning slightly out of tune and "oozing" into the unison. This also works well with repeated patterns.

--- Drones -- using an open string along with a fingered string. This is usually associated with country and Cajun style fiddling. Some of that music has a strong connection to the Blues. (Look at the Bluegrass section for an example.)

Try these following double stops. I used the two very different keys of D and B♭ (next page). "P.T." means *passing tone,* notes that aren't in the chord.

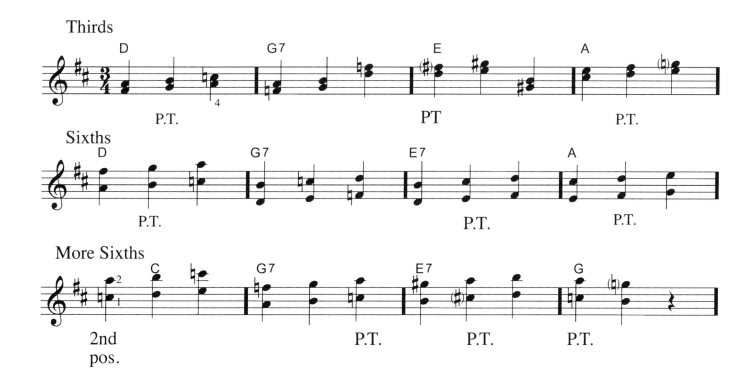

59

These diminished 5th double stops contain the 3rd and ♭7th of the chord.
You have to "squish" the fingers together to get these in tune.

Use the same fingers and slide--try this with all of the dim. 5 double stops.

in B♭

Double Stop Shuffle

Marty Laster

This is two parts -- first in the key of A and then in C.

Yodeling Licks - This relates to double stops in the following way:

Take the following double stops in G:

You can create a yodeling lick by arpeggiating (bracket) and adding a passing tone (p.t.):

Or you could try it this way

Try going up-in D:

Transposing to other keys is fairly simple -- just begin on the third of the
new key, jump up a sixth and continue the pattern. First chord is the V (dominant).

Yodeling Licks are usually associated with country music, but can come in handy for comic relief in a swing tune and are great practice in overall technique.

The use of the **Interval of the 7th** in the Blues is technically difficult, but can be very effective. It is by nature, dissonant and the level of that dissonance will vary, depending on a few factors. The Major 7th is, of course the most jarring interval (used mostly in minor keys) in addition to the use of the 9th. Sometimes this technique can be used to create the equivalent of an exclamation point. It's difficult to get in tune and often can only be played in third position. Try these examples in a few keys and sample improv. so you can see how it works. Notice the suspensions that can resolve from the 7th to the 6th.

The interval written above some of the sevenths refers to the upper note's function in scale.

Here's a sample of an improv using some 7th double stops. I moved to G to give you more practice in various keys. This is an 8-bar blues.

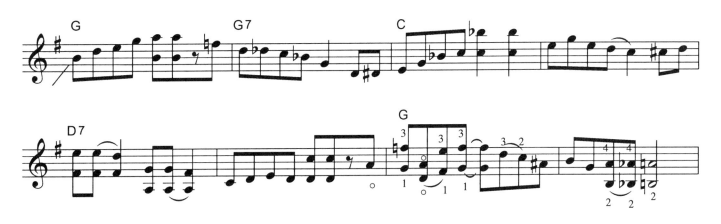

Try these suspensions that resolve (bracket.)

63

The Master Blues Scale

This is the scale that contains all the "Blue" notes and the chordal ones. You may say this is the entire palette of sounds used in the blues. I'll show you the scale in three keys. Aside from blues in a bebop jazz or fusion context, you won't often find all these notes in a blues setting, but it's good to see what the possibilities are. The cluster of chromatic notes are shown with brackets.
The chameleon is decked out in full color for this one.

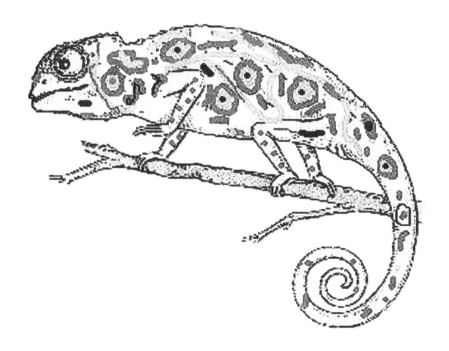

Chromatic Notes
-- These are the notes played in half steps that often don't fall into the scales or chords. In the history of the blues, the heavy use of chromatics came into being about the time of bebop jazz, in which the Blues continued to have a central role. Look at the beginning of "Blue Monk," written by the great Thelonious Monk, for a good example of the use of these chromatics in an easy-going tempo. The brackets show these non-chordal notes.

Let's experiment by playing a variation of the first two measures of "Blue Monk" and then adding two measures of new chromatic ideas. Sorry, Thelonious. On the CD, this is preceded by the "Master Blues Scale," in one key.

65

Here's a blues tune of my own that is chock full of chromaticism.
It's in a quasi-bebop style; I'll call it...

Chro-Magnon Man

Marty Laster

Look at the third measure from the end. This lick is influenced by the bluegrass style. I'm adding a note for resolution. Here are two possible fingerings. The first is good for sliding in a slower tempo and the second....well, you guessed it.

66

Lower Neighbor Tones

This refers to the use of the note a half step below a chordal note, which then resolves to the chordal or arpeggio tone. I am using the G7 arpeggio (G, B, D, F) to demonstrate this. Vertical lines point out these tones.

This is followed by a blues tune in swing style to demonstrate this technique.

(Note: Lower neighbors are not to be confused with downstairs neighbors.)

This involves circling the neighbor note in eighth notes or triplets

 Here's a blues tune that uses these neighboring tones. We'll call it...

Good Neighbors

Marty Laster

67

Here's a favorite technique, mostly used in swing style. I'll call this 3-note pattern "the sandwich."
The order of the notes is as follows:
1) upper neighbor
2) lower neighbor
3) the chordal note-vertical line
Note - The lower neighbor is always a half step from chordal note.

Now try this one. It's now a four-note pattern in which every other note is the chordal (arpeggio) tone.
Order is now:
1) upper neighbor
2) arpeggio
3) lower neighbor
4) arpeggio

Here's one more. This one's a bit trickier and involves two chordal tones:
1) lower neighbor
2) chordal note
3) upper neighbor of next chordal note up
4) new chordal note

Practice these in the following keys until it's second nature.
E, A, D, G, C, F, B♭, E♭

We'll combine all these neighboring ideas into this swing-style blues entitled...

Better Neighbors

Marty Laster

Of course, a real break would have more breathing time (less notes) but I wanted to fit in as many examples of neighbors as I could in this one. These techniques work well in Swing as well as in Blues. Get these in your fingertips by practicing in all keys. The grueling practice will pay off.

Here I tried to put all the neighboring ideas in one musical phrase, with a couple of small variations. This is all over a G chord.

Rhythm 3 - Let's see how your skill with reading and feeling complex rhythms is progressing. This next section combines syncopations and much of the rhythms we will need. First try these with a metronome.

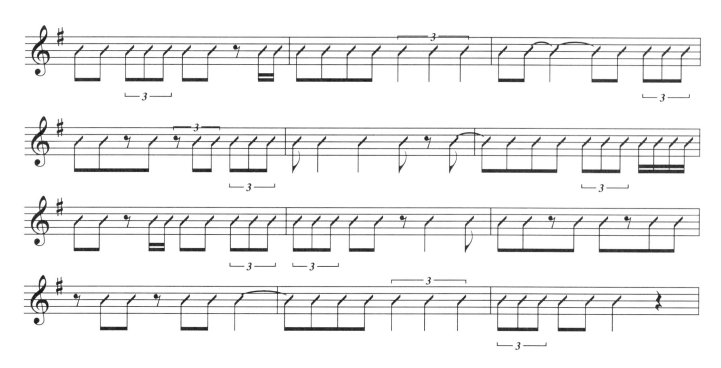

This is a blues break based on the above rhythms. Keep that metronome handy. This isn't easy.

Microtones -- Playing in the "Twilight Zone"

It is interesting to realize that the amount of space between say, a D note and a C♯, a half step down can be seen as infinite: Let me explain. Slide your finger down halfway (50%) between the D and the C♯ with the 3rd finger. That's called a quarter-tone. Then do it again (eighth tone). You can do this endlesslessly without ever reaching the C♯. This is sometimes called micro-tonality. With the blues, let's just call it "getting funky." It is fun getting lost in the cracks and occasionally someone falls in, never to be seen again. This is one of the unfortunate risks of playing the blues.

Keep in mind that before the well-tempered system of music began in the 18th century, the con-cept of octaves divided into 12 equal parts was unheard of. Also in other cultures, notably India, microtones are common. This is a technique used a lot by electric guitarists who aren't condi-tioned by classical training and is an incredibly expressive rock technique as well.

This is very difficult to notate, but here's an example of microtonality (or, fiddlin' in the "Twilight Zone"). This goes from a B to a B♭. Each note is a hair lower until you reach the B♭, but if you don't quite reach it, that's alright.

71

Photograph courtesy of Old Hat Records

The Black String Band Tradition

There is a detailed history of this largely lost tradition in the booklet that comes with the CD, *Violin, Sing the Blues for Me*, on the Old Hat label. This was a vibrant musical world in the south that, unfortunately isn't reflected in the recording industry. There are names of many fiddlers that I saw for the first time in the above text.

It is documented (for what it's worth) that during the slave era, fiddlers were often given special treatment. Homemade instruments were common and there was tremendous variety, stylistically, in the music. From the late 1800s into the 1940s bands, as now, played what they needed to in order to make ends meet and to get into closed doors. The repertoire of these string bands consisted of southern old-timey tunes, ragtime, novelty tunes and of course, the blues. There was a revival of some of this "jug band" music in the '60s, and often there was a tub-bass added as a novelty instrument. In actuality, that instrument began out of dire poverty and was also easier to travel with than a double bass.

Try to get *Violin, Sing the Blues for Me*. It is rich in history and great music.

Let's next pay tribute to some of the great blues and swing violinists, both alive and dead. They all live on in their recordings and what they have taught us.

Photograph courtesy of Old Hat Records

73

Howard Armstrong was an important figure in the early development of blues and jazz violin. But he was much more than that, being a multi-linguist and an artist. His drawing on the cover of the LP, *The Barnyard Dance* (Martin, Bogan and Armstrong) is brilliant. If you get this as a CD, you're really missing out. He played the eclectic styles of the black string bands of the 20s and 30s. Blues was mixed with ragtime, novelty tunes (probably influenced by Vaudeville) and southern old-timey style. His playing was soulful and chock-full of slides and basic blues licks, but improvisation was on the simple side in today's standards. Armstrong's earlier bands were (in the '30s) the Four Aces and the Tennessee Chocolate Drops but he is largely known for his work with Carl Martin and Ted Bogan. He played with them into the '70s and kept the tradition alive. The CD example in this book ("Vine Street Drag") was played by the Tennessee Drops and can be found on the CD, *Violin, Sing the Blues for Me*, You can hear in this excerpt a blues lick that I believe influenced the development of early bluegrass fiddling style.

Papa John Creach was possibly the first blues violinist to play in a rock context. He was known for his work in Hot Tuna, Jefferson Airplane and Jefferson Starship. Two aspects of his blues playing that stand out are his extensive use of slides and his wild, but controlled vibrato, which gave his playing a lot of character. The violin in a rock context had a novelty appeal in the early '70s but Creach helped pave the way for a more respectable view of the instrument.

Eddie South was a violinist of extraordinary talent who never received the acclaim he deserved, at least not in the United States. Having achieved virtuosity as a classical player at a young age, he, as a black musician had tremendous difficulty getting recognition in what was then a largely racist society. He then moved into the jazz world and gained great respect, especially overseas. He stayed in Budapest for quite a while and absorbed the Gypsy music influences there. Eventually he teamed up with the great Gypsy guitarist Django Reinhardt and did some of his best playing at that time. Of course it was Stephane Grappelli who had also been playing with Django in the Hot Club of France.

I bring up Eddie South in the context of a book on blues for a specific reason. In ballads, his Gypsy technique of sliding slowly into notes was so incredibly soulful that I feel that there was no need for the blues scale. Playing the melody with slides was sufficient for South. Again, it was the *journey* of the slide that was important, not getting to the next note. Try to get the LP (or CD) of *Eddie South, The Dark Angel of the Violin*, to hear an example of his incredible tone and sliding technique. He plays great, up tempo swing on this album as well, but for our purposes, we'll stay with the ballad.

Stuff Smith had that perfect blend of blues and an almost demonic swing feel in his playing. He sang with the same gutsy style as he played. Early in his career, Stuff played relatively complex clarinet lines while his later work evolved into a more sparse, trumpet like attack, with traces of Bebop phrasing. He only used about 6 inches of bow and said "I only use a few inches of my bow, where I have better control - like a trumpeter controls his breathing."

Son of a barber-musician, Smith learned violin with his father. When he heard the trumpeter, Louie Armstrong, he moved from classical music to jazz. He played with Jelly Roll Morton, but eventually formed his own quintet, which was a sensation at the Onyx Club on 52nd Street (New York) in the 1930s. Jascha Heifetz and Fritz Kreisler would come and listen and there was mutual admiration between them. In 1936, Stuff Smith became the first violinist to play an electric violin. Stuff was known as being friendly and always ready with a joke, in addition to being hard working and dependable.

He was known to use parallel fifths in his playing. Try this: Put your finger on two strings at once (a double stop using one finger) and play a scale. How Stuff made this work musically is baffling.

(Don) Sugarcane Harris was a great blues/rock and fusion violinist. He played straight forward blues, but was best known for his playing in fusion style in which a single chord would be held "'til the cows come home", while Sugarcane would play a collage of virtuostic patterns, repeated licks and fast scale passages. His electric violin at times sounded like a guitar and his held trills emulated the harmonica. "Sugarcane" was known for his work with Frank Zappa (*Hot Rats* album), John Mayall, Little Richard, and others. He inspired many with his approach to the blues and flawless technique.

When **Jean-Luc Ponty** hit the jazz scene in the '60s, he was immediately an innovative force. He began with classical studies at a young age and was accepted within a couple of years into a major orchestra. During that time, he was jamming late night in jazz clubs. He couldn't do it all, so Ponty committed himself to fusion jazz. Drawn to the sounds of John Coltrane and Miles Davis, Ponty began to adapt bebop phrasing to his own playing. Teaming up in 1969 with Frank Zappa, he continued to explore rhythmic and other musical ideas. His extensive use of electronic effects that often disguise the sound of the violin, in addition to his virtuosity and compositional skills, began to set him apart from other jazz violinists of the time. Also, having moved into world music and African rhythms, the repeated licks and patterns used have become quite complex. This can be heard on his recording, *Tchokola*. Ponty continues to be a creative force in the new millennium.

Vassar Clements

Tim Owen

Tim Owen

In Memoriam

Vassar Clements established himself as an icon in the fiddling world. He died on August 16th 2005 at the age of 77 and we mourn his passing. Vassar's musical world encompassed bluegrass, country, rock, blues, jazz, and swing styles. He was a virtuoso player who stretched his ideas to the limit while staying true to the feel of the style being played.

At an early age, Vassar was highly influenced by the big band swing sounds around him. At the age of 14 he played bluegrass with Bill Monroe and later with Jim and Jesse McReynolds. After a break from music, Vassar moved to Nashville and played with John Hartford and the Earl Scruggs Review. He then recorded on the milestone recording, *Will the Circle be Unbroken* with the Nitty Gritty Dirt Band. It is here that I first heard Vassar and was mesmerized by his playing. This (double) album also helped introduce a whole new generation to bluegrass music. He than played with the Grateful Dead and recorded and toured with Old and in the Way with Jerry Garcia on banjo (from the Grateful Dead).

Vassar's playing showed tremendous blues influence and his extensive use of slides was a trademark. Listen to his last CD, *"Living the Blues"*.

Vassar Clements was known as a gentleman with humility and a generous spirit. Few fiddlers today have not been influenced by his expressive tone and original, bluesy licks - that live on in our playing and in our memories.

Scroll of Vassar's Violin

Ronald Sachs

Honorable Mention

The following jazz/blues violinists deserve mention for their great contribution to the world of music.
Sorry I couldn't devote a page to each of them and my apologies to those I may have left out

Stephane Grappelli   Joe Venuti
Claude Williams   John Blake
Svend Asmussen   Leroy Jenkins
Johnny Gimble   Michael Urbaniak
Ray Nance

All due respect to the countless blues artists of other instruments
Here are a few.

Guitar

B.B. King   Muddy Waters   Eric Clapton
John Lee Hooker   Johnnie Winters   George Benson
Jimi Hendrix - More than a psychedelic rock star - give a closer listen.
Buddy Guy - Great player who influenced Hendrix
Robert Johnson - Great singer and Delta Blues player.
Taj Mahal - Multi instrumentalist, singer and historian

Paul Butterfield, Phil Wiggins and countless others - Harmonica (Harp)

Count Basie, James P. Johnson, Art Tatum,
Albert Ammons - Keyboard

Bessie Smith, Billie Holiday – Vocalists
Maria Muldaur can also sing some great blues.

The list is endless.

About Making Music

This is the last and possibly the most important part of this book. In some ways, it's the hardest lesson to teach and requires the most patience on the part of the student. For some of you gifted souls and genius types, these concepts will be obvious, but for most of us they will take a bit of slow, hard work. The reward is the ability to express and communicate your feelings fully and freely through music without thinking about it.

Our goal is for improvisation to flow like speech, with a natural sense of tension and release. We are uncomfortable listening to someone talk who speaks fast and nonstop. We also fall asleep to a monotonous voice and are impatient with s l o w   s p e e c h. Also, a lack of humor or constant intensity on one hand and superficial, muzak-like playing can be annoying. The same is true with music. Let's examine the ways to build and vary a break to keep the interest of the listener. Also, don't forget the concept of music as sound sculpture, where rests are not a break from the music, but an integral part of it.

It can be argued, if one plays what they feel, how can you say there's a right or wrong. It's not a question of right and wrong, it's one of better and worse.

Igor Stravinsky wrote in his book, *The Poetics of Music*, that there's no freedom without discipline. It's a remarkable concept. After applying the following ideas to your playing to the point where they are automatic, you can still play what you feel but it will be more articulate. Excuse the lecturing tone but I feel strongly about this stuff. Let's look now at the different ways to vary and develop a break, one at a time. We'll define break as any improvisation, whether in blues, swing or another style.

1) Register - One way to vary a break is to begin in your lower register and work your way up. Playing on the E string generally cuts through and is more intense than the G and D strings so you may want to end on a high note.

Beginning softly and building in volume can also be effective.

Think of it as a long crescendo from pp to FF.

(Note: All these rules can be broken - 3rd position or 5th position on the G string can be very intense and after climaxing on the E string, you may want to go back to the G and end on a mellow note. The ways to create a great break are endless. Use these ideas as a jumping off point.)

2) Call and Response - This relates to register. You would play a line or lick in one register and answer it in another.

3) Slow and Fast -- Going from sustained tones to fast moving ones can be an effective way of varying a break and creating tension-release.

4) A similar idea is the use of patterns of repeated notes followed by free movement, giving the impression of having been stuck or trapped and then released or liberated. The last example (3) does this in the 2nd to the 3rd measure. Here's another example:

Repeated pattern - Entrapment   Liberation

5) Going from small intervals to large ones also can give the feeling of things opening up or having more breathing space.

6) Wall of sound to more rests - Let's start the same way.

The wall   Ah! I could breathe.

7) Straight rhythm vs. syncopation - Suddenly you feel off center.

Straight- Grounded   - - - - - - - - - - - - - - Syncopation- Vertigo

8) Non-bluesy notes (consonance) to bluesy (dissonant) - Gives the impression that life is good and happy and then suddenly there's trouble brewing.

9) Soft and loud - This speaks for itself and is a great way to add life and drama to your break (also called dynamics). It works great when changing chords. This also works well with call and response (Try this with the #2 example).

10) Weaving out - last but not least; take a short musical statement, repeat while adding a few more notes. Do this again. It is similar to speech.

I am going home, I am going home to eat I'm going home to eat and have a beer to wash it all down.

You can see that the possibilities for ideas in improvising are endless. My goal here is to jump start you into exploring all the possibilities.

Now let's put all these ideas into a pair of blues breaks. In reality, you would never try to cram all these techniques into a solo. You can play a great break using one or two of these concepts. I put the number of each technique next to the measure it begins and a dotted line above or below to show the length. There are sometimes 2 numbers due to the overlapping of these ideas. This is now in the key of G.

Some General Tips

About Pickups- it's largely a matter of taste. I prefer a natural violin sound and like the L.R. Baggs bridge pickup and preamp. Also, David Gage makes a very even sounding and sensitive pickup that fits under the bridge. Some prefer the electric sound and prefer a Zeta or other solid body violin. Hand carved solid wooden violins may give a warmer tone and can also qualify as works of art.

Joe Venuti had a characteristic tone on what I believe was a DeArmond pickup. I believe they were the first ones and I never liked the sound, but hey! - it was still Joe Venuti and few questioned his tone. He actually continued playing on this pickup after the Barcus Berry was introduced. Enter Jon-Luc Ponty with his state-of-the-art MIDI-technology and all the sound effect pedals, and a world of new possibilities was opened up.

Sometimes the tone required can be dictated by the nature of the playing situation and it may be good to have both a good acoustic and electric setup.

The 5-string violin offers the low viola C string and the range is impressive. Good acoustic 5-strings are hard to come by and a small, converted viola can fit the bill.

About amplifiers- make sure that the bass response is good. Many guitar amps favor the high (treble) end. An amp with a large speaker (16" or 20") is preferable. You may consider a separate speaker from the amp (head). Also, consider using a pre-amp and/or an equalizer. A 7-band EQ pedal has saved me more than once; especially if you are forced to play through a tiny amp.

About Technical Proficiency- you can be a pretty good blues player without it, but you will be held back from fully expressing your ideas. Good bow technique and intonation should be sought after and taking a few lessons with an open-minded classical teacher may be a good idea.

About the bow- until recently, I never paid attention to bow quality. What a difference a good bow makes to our playing. Some like the newer carbon fiber ones and the decision is very personal. And even if you are playing on a $200 violin, you may decide to pay much more than that on the right bow. However, without good bowing technique, you may not feel much difference between a $20 and a $2000 bow.

About reading music- This (obviously) will not make you a great player, but in today's day and age one needs to be prepared for someone throwing a written tune in front of you and asking you to sight-read it. I feel it's a necessary skill.

A Special Note:

The Grimace– While playing the blues, one should wear a facial expression contorted with pain, passion, and generalized angst. This is particularly effective while bending notes, but don't overdo. This will surely lead to more and higher paying gigs.

For playing swing, a mildly silly grin is in order and for blues in swing style- no expression at all is appropriate. While playing bluegrass- the stoic, stone face look is the way to go.

Trouble in Mind

as played by Phil Wiggins- (Alligator Records) (harmonica) of Cephas and Wiggins.

I love this short, tasteful break. It first states the melody 1), then the E blues scale 2). Next he stretches out with some triplet figures 3) and ends on the dominant chord in the lower register 4).

85

Blues for the Road

I thought I'd leave you with a couple of classic old blues tunes.
These are great to jam to and good to have in your repertoire.
Have a good time with the...

St. James Infirmary

This next classic, was written by the great Bessie Smith. Bessie was a master at bending notes and singing in the cracks. That made it hard to transcribe this. It's amazing what she did with 3 or 4 notes - classic Blues style. Here is the ---

St. Louis Blues

Bessie Smith

The Blues

The Afro-American musical experience was a synthesis of African tradition with European harmonies and American folk idioms. Add to this, individual talent and the depth of feeling associated with the experience of slavery and you come up a uniquely American musical style that we call the blues.

Now here's a provocative question. Do other countries and cultures besides our own play a form of the blues? Well, if style takes a back seat to how the music makes us feel, the answer may be yes. Let's explore this some more.

Taking another culture rich with it's own package of strengths and abilities and add suffering of other, (not necessarily equal) forms of persecution, you will come up with a unique expression of music (or art.) However, if you close your eyes and listen for a long time, the feelings engendered may be surprisingly similar to the blues.

Listen to an Irish air played by the Uillean pipes. Just the sound of that instrument playing modal melodies with a yearning quality can be quite moving. How about a slow Klezmer tune with the ornamentation and augmented intervals? Have you heard the simple, but haunting Andean tunes with instrumental combinations found only in that culture? On the other extreme, enter Ludvig Von Beethoven. In the hands of a great composer, who lost his hearing at a young age you find incredible soul. When I am feeling down, I may one day listen to some blues and the next, a Beethoven string quartet. Each is liberating in its own way. When we come down to it, it's not style that defines greatness; it's the individual artist's ability and expression. All great music can be full of painful feelings and at the same time be life affirming and even joyous. This is what the blues has in common with the other world music styles I mentioned.

Does this mean that we can call it all the blues? OF COURSE NOT! The blues is one of the few indigenous art forms of our young country and we can take deep pride in that.

The point I am making is, just as various languages can express the entire spectrum of human emotions, so do the languages of music. In other words, we're all in this together (spoken by a true child of the 60s). So now our chameleon is not only changing color (dialect), but form as well (language) and may be disguised as a duck, grasshopper, or a platypus. In any case, let's toast to the Blues and to its extended family as well.

(Yes, I have been watching you, on and off.) I am impressed with your progress but you still need some practice in the key of E♭, Then again, don't we all.

Marty Laster

The swamp's dried up
 I'm sleeping on rocks
  My body's cold and sore
   My baby's gone, she took all my clothes
    I can't blend into this world no more

Ain't caught a fly in a month
 I'm tired and hungry
  Don't know what to do, I've got
   arthritis, bursitis, insomnia, psychosis
    I got the right to sing the Blues

I would like to thank the following people for their help with this book: Andy Polon and Peter Ecklund for sharing their vast blues and swing knowledge; Phil Schneider, Alan Laster and my wife Jackie for their support. A big thank you goes out to Angelo DeCesare for his brilliant fiddling crawfish and helmet cartoons and to my son, Michael, who enhanced them on Photoshop. Here's to my students who, unknowingly, became guinea pigs for my working out some of these ideas. Thanks to Lisa Gutkin for her great playing on the CD and in helping to proofread the music. Last but not least, let's give gratitude to all of the great musicians and composers, living or not, who inspire, move, and teach us.

Marty Laster
(martylaster.com)

I welcome your comments.